1. Ru

Biography

Y0-EGI-512

AMERICAN
RACE CAR DRIVERS

The Racing Books

AMERICAN
RACE CAR DRIVERS

MARK DILLON

Lerner Publications Company ■ Minneapolis, Minnesota

ACKNOWLEDGMENTS: The illustrations are reproduced through the courtesy of: pp. 4, 12, 15, 30, United Press International; pp. 6 (top), 32, 50, 51, Goodyear Tire and Rubber Company; p. 6 (bottom), United States Automobile Club; pp. 7, 20, 21, 26, 31, National Association for Stock Car Auto Racing, Incorporated; pp. 9, 42, 45, 46, 49, Roger Penske Enterprises, Incorporated; pp. 11, 19, 35, Firestone Tire and Rubber Company; pp. 13, 48, Wide World Photos; pp. 17, 34, 36 (top and bottom), 41, Indianapolis Motor Speedway; pp. 23, 39, Sport Photographic; pp. 25, 28, Vernon Biever; p. 27, Independent Picture Service; p. 44, General Graphic.

LIBRARY OF CONGRESS CATALOGING IN PUBLICATION DATA

Dillon, Mark.
    American race car drivers.

    (The Racing Books)
    SUMMARY: Describes the lives and the racing careers of four well-known American race car drivers: Parnelli Jones, Richard Petty, A. J. Foyt, and Mark Donohue.

    1. Automobile racing—Biography—Juvenile literature. [1. Automobile racing—Biography] I. Title.

GV1032.A1D54   796.7'2'0922 [B] [92]   73-22511
ISBN 0-8225-0409-X

Published simultaneously in Canada by J. M. Dent & Sons Ltd., Don Mills, Ontario.

Manufactured in the United States of America.

International Standard Book Number: 0-8225-0409-X
Library of Congress Catalog Card Number: 73-22511

INTRODUCTION

A.J. Foyt, Mark Donohue, Parnelli Jones, and Richard Petty have all had dazzling careers in automobile racing. Most of these men are still leading contenders in racing events. But the road to success for each one of them has been long, dangerous, and fiercely competitive. As professionals who have made racing their way of life, these drivers give their all to win. They are well aware that at any moment during a race their lives could end violently due to the slightest mistake in judgment. Yet each driver is determined not only to race against these odds but also to *win*. It is this devotion to racing despite the danger that makes professional race-car drivers a special breed.

The four famous American race-car drivers included in this book have gained fame in either track or road racing, or both. Track racing, as the name suggests, is conducted on an oval-shaped dirt or asphalt track. In track racing, many cars compete at the same time in close formation while traveling at high speeds. The challenge in track racing is to maneuver the car into a first-place position without running into other cars or the track wall.

Road racing is conducted on courses designed to include the same driving conditions found on regular roads. In contrast to an oval-shaped track, a road course is irregularly shaped because it is made up of a series of curves. A road course has uphill and downhill grades, variations in light and shade (if there are trees along the course), and occasionally variations in road surface. The challenge of road racing lies in the driver's ability to maneuver his car over the hills and around the curves in order to gain position. And he must accomplish all of this while traveling at tremendous speeds. Not only is the driver's judgment and driving skill tested, but the car's handling ability and endurance are also put to a severe test.

There are three basic racing cars that operate on oval-track and road courses. These are open-wheel cars, stock cars, and sports cars. Open-wheel cars are single-seat racers that have no fenders covering the wheels. The big championship cars that compete at the Indianapolis Speedway are one type of open-wheel car. Because they compete in America's most important championship-car race, the Indianapolis 500, these cars are also called "Indy cars". The United States Auto Club (USAC) sanctions, or approves, championship-car racing in America and awards a national championship title to the leading driver in each of its four race-car divisions— sprint, midget, stock, and championship car.

Another type of open-wheel car is the

An Indianapolis championship car

Midget racers

"formula" car, a powerful racing car that looks like an Indy car but is built for road racing. There is a strict formula, or set of rules, controlling its weight, design, and engine size. The biggest and fastest formula cars are the Formula 1 cars. Formula 1 cars are featured in the international Grand Prix races.

The third type of open-wheel racer includes the midget and sprint cars. These cars are smaller versions of the championship, or Indy, cars. Midget- and sprint-car races are run on dirt or asphalt tracks and are sanctioned by USAC.

Stock cars are track-racing cars. They look like standard passenger cars, but they have been modified in various ways for racing.

A stock car

Many young race drivers start their racing careers in jalopies—beat-up old cars. Jalopies are raced on dirt tracks and frequently take a beating as they crash into each other during a race. The finest cars in the stock-car class are those that are more highly modified for maximum performance. These cars also have extra safety features, such as automatic fire extinguishers, crash-resistant fuel tanks, and reinforced doors. These are the cars that run in the Grand National races sponsored by the National Association of Stock Car Auto Racing (NASCAR). NASCAR is the major sponsoring organization in stock-car racing. It sponsors the famous Daytona 500 and other Grand National stock-car races. Points earned in these races can lead to a national championship title awarded by NASCAR to the leading point holder.

Sports cars are road-racing machines. These cars are powerful, two-seated vehicles with fenders, windshields, and other features that are standard on regular street-model cars. These "production" sports cars are made for general street use; they are also modified for racing on road courses. Sports-racing cars, on the other hand, are specially designed for racing on road courses. Among the best known production sports cars are the MG, Triumph, Porsche, and Chevrolet Corvette. Some of the best known names among sports-racing cars are the McLaren, Lola, and Eagle.

Amateur and professional sports-car races in this country are sanctioned by the Sports Car Club of America (SCCA) and are held on road courses all over the United States. In America, several professional sports-car series are sanctioned by SCCA. One of these is the Canadian-American Challenge Cup (Can-Am) for big sports-racing cars like McLarens and Lolas. Another series is the Trans-American Sedan Championship (Trans-Am) for sports sedans like Mustangs,

A sports sedan

Camaros, AMX Javelins, and smaller sedans like Alfa-Romeo and Datsun. The L&M Continental 5000 series is also sanctioned by SCCA. This series is for single-seat, open-wheel formula cars. One of the most famous sports-car races of all is not associated with SCCA. That race is the 24-hour endurance run held every year at LeMans, France.

These then are the races, race cars, and race-car divisions in which Foyt, Donohue, Jones, and Petty have become expert drivers. In the following pages, you will read about how these men got started in racing and how their careers developed.

PARNELLI JONES

Dirt-track racing has often been called the backbone of American auto racing because it has served as a proving ground for so many prominent American race drivers. During the 1950s, dirt-track racing was especially big, for that was the decade that produced many of America's most famous race-car drivers. One of those drivers was Parnelli Jones.

Born in 1933 in Texarcana, Arkansas, Rufus Parnel Jones grew up in southern California. He was interested in cars at the age of 12, but he was even more interested in horses. So he found work in a nearby stable and saved enough money to buy himself a horse. However, by the time Parnelli got his driver's license at 16, he had become fascinated by cars. By swapping his old interest for his new one, Parnelli literally horse-traded his way into his first car, an early-model hot-rod Ford. Along with some friends, who had nick-named him "Parnelli," he raced his Ford every chance he got. Racing cars eventually became so important to him that he dropped out of high school to work full-time in a garage. He was now saving money to buy a jalopy for dirt-track racing. Within a short time, he acquired one and began entering his first dirt-track races.

From the time Parnelli Jones started racing at 17, he was a real "charger" on the track. He was not very large—five feet seven, 170 pounds—but he could handle a heavy jalopy as well as anyone else. Apart from his skill, it was his daring and aggressive driving style that gradually earned him a reputation on the dirt tracks. Often rolling his car, Jones took a lot of chances in his all-out efforts to win. He knew he had to beat some tough competition in order to win recognition. And winning the prize money could help a lot, too, since maintenance of a car was so expensive.

Fortunately, Parnelli got a break early in his racing career when a California auto wrecker, Omar Danielson, saw him race in 1954. Danielson liked the young man's determination, so he decided to let Jones race one of his own cars. (In other words, Danielson would take care of expenses.) But Danielson's friends warned him that Jones was a troublemaker and therefore a poor risk. This accusation was only partly true. Jones *was* rolling cars and getting into frequent fistfights, but he was also winning races. And winning was the important thing. Because Danielson had a lot of confidence in Jones, he became the young man's first sponsor, or financial backer.

During the late 1950s, Parnelli graduated from jalopies to the faster, more powerful midget and sprint cars. In order to race in the sprint-car circuit, he joined the International

Parnelli Jones

In the mad frenzy of dirt-track racing, jalopies often roll out
of control on a fast curve, or crash and turn end over end.

Motor Contest Association (IMCA), an organization that sponsored sprint-car races all over the country. Driving for Danielson and a new sponsor, Harlan Fike, Parnelli began to make a name for himself as he moved from the race tracks of California to the midwestern and eastern tracks of IMCA. In competition, Parnelli was beginning to mature as a driver, frequently winning over big-name drivers. But the greatest indication of his growing success was an offer of membership from the United States Automobile Club. USAC was then, and still is today, one of the most important auto-racing clubs in the country. So when Parnelli was invited to join USAC, he knew what an opportunity it was. In 1960, after watching USAC's Indianapolis 500, Parnelli decided to join the "big time." He left IMCA for USAC, and drove in its sprint-car division.

Parnelli Jones won 7 out of 13 sprint-car

Parnelli Jones climbs out of his racer after a good practice lap before the 1961 Indy 500. Car owner J. C. Agajanian stands at the far right.

races during the 1960 USAC racing season, an achievement that earned him the USAC Midwest Sprint Car Championship. A year later, when USAC discontinued regional championships in favor of national titles, Parnelli won the national crown. Astonishing everyone, he repeated this performance again in 1962, becoming the first driver to win three consecutive sprint-car crowns.

After 1961, Parnelli Jones became a nationally recognized racing figure. Not only was he the country's sprint-car champion, but he had also made a favorable showing in his first Indianapolis 500-mile race. In 1961, wealthy race promoter J.C. "Aggie" Agajanian had provided Parnelli with a championship car for the Indy 500 race. Though Parnelli led the race for the first 27 laps, mechanical problems forced him to finish 12th overall. But it had been a good performance, and it earned Jones the Rookie of the Year award. For the remainder of the racing season, Parnelli racked up more wins in the sprint-car circuit. He also ventured into driving sports cars and stock cars, becoming as skillful with them as he was with sprint cars.

At the 1962 Indy race, Parnelli qualified for the pole position (the number-one spot in the starting line-up) with a record speed of 150 mph. Unfortunately, his car developed brake trouble during the race and finished seventh. The big car was the same one that Parnelli had driven in his previous Indy race. A big front-engined roadster nicknamed "Ol' Calhoun," it was typical of the other Indy cars. Though Ol' Calhoun was beginning to show its age, Parnelli and Aggie decided to keep it for the 1963 Indy race.

In 1963, the Europeans came to Indianapolis with five European road-racing cars made by the Lotus company of England. Lotus modified their cars especially for track racing at Indy. Controversy immediately boiled up among the Indy drivers because they resented the intrusion of the European cars. The Indy Speedway, they declared, had always been a race track for front-engined roadsters. The Lotus cars, on the other hand, were rear-engined machines, much lower, lighter, and faster than the front-engined Indy cars. Furthermore, the European "funny cars," as the Indy regulars named them, required fewer pit stops for fuel and tire changes than the Indy roadsters. It looked as if the 1963 Indy 500 would be a battle between the two car classes. Parnelli and Aggie agreed that only an all-out effort by the roadsters could defeat the Lotus cars.

His car's fuel tank on fire, Jones leaps for his life during a refueling mishap. This accident cost him the lead in the 1964 Indy 500.

For the second year in a row, Parnelli qualified for the pole position in the starting line-up. At the green flag, Parnelli pulled out in first place ahead of Jim Clark, Grand Prix champion. Keeping the lead, Parnelli increased the pace with every lap. It looked as though Ol' Calhoun had it won when, late in the race, a crack developed in the car's outside oil tank. As the track became slick with the leaking oil, the race officials prepared to signal Parnelli off the track. But Agajanian convinced them that the leak would stop when the oil level dropped below the crack in the tank. It did. Only slightly in the lead at race's end, Parnelli whipped across the finish line just ahead of Jim Clark in a Lotus-Ford. Parnelli Jones had finally won the Indianapolis 500, and with an Indy roadster, too. Despite the victory, however, the race clearly revealed that the heavy roadsters were no match for the new rear-engined lightweights.

In 1964, Parnelli tried one of the new lightweights but didn't like it. So he returned to his faithful roadster for the year's Indy 500. Although the car had been extensively reworked for the race, Parnelli could only manage to finish 23rd. Another driver, A.J. Foyt, won the race, driving a roadster. Though the roadsters had triumphed again, 1964 proved to be the last year for them as Indy cars. So Parnelli and Aggie bought a Lotus-Ford for the 1965 Indy, realizing that it was their only chance to win. Parnelli still

did not feel comfortable in a Lotus, but he did manage to finish in second place behind Jim Clark's Lotus. The Lotus car had finally replaced the Indy roadster at the Indianapolis Speedway.

Aside from racing at Indy, Parnelli Jones was active in USAC's sports- and stock-car competitions. Proving his ability to win major auto races of *any* kind, he won the USAC stock-car title in 1964, and the California Grand Prix for sports cars in 1965.

By 1966, after 16 years of auto racing, Parnelli Jones was financially very well off. He had wisely invested his winnings in various businesses, including a Firestone tire distributorship. And he also had some land investments. Because his ventures were doing so well, money was no longer the motivation for racing that it had been in the past. So in 1966, Parnelli decided to cut down on his racing and enter only the major race-car events.

A year later, Parnelli was lured back to

Parnelli Jones at Indianapolis in the STP Turbocar, 1967

Indianapolis by an exciting offer from race sponsor Andy Granatelli. Granatelli had built a revolutionary new racing car, and he invited Jones to drive it at the 1967 Indy 500. The new "Turbocar" had a turbine engine that was faster and more powerful than the internal-combustion engines of the other Indy cars. At the time trials, the Turbocar proved to be the car to beat. Some drivers, including A.J. Foyt, felt that the Turbocar had an unfair advantage over the other Indy cars. But despite arguments, the race went on as usual. At the green flag, Parnelli zoomed off in the Turbocar. He easily led the entire race until the final laps. Unexpectedly, a six-dollar part in the car's transmission broke, costing Jones the victory. Jones was again offered the Turbocar for the 1968 Indy 500, but he turned down the offer. Joe Leonard drove the Turbocar instead, and led the entire race only to break down, as Parnelli had, just a few laps from victory.

Parnelli Jones never returned to Indianapolis as a driver after 1967. Instead, he bought and managed his own team of Indy cars, hiring drivers Mario Andretti, Al Unser, and Joe Leonard, among others. Since becoming an owner, Parnelli Jones has won the Indianapolis 500 two years in a row—1970 and 1971. Both victories were won by driver Al Unser.

Parnelli Jones has not retired from racing completely. He has driven Ford Mustangs with a great deal of success in the Sports Car Club of America's Trans-American Sedan Championship (Trans-Am) series. In 1970, Parnelli won five Trans-Am races in a Ford Mustang to capture the Trans-Am title.

In addition to sports-car racing, Jones' other major racing interest is off-road racing. In off-road racing, dune-buggies, motorcycles, and four-wheel drive vehicles compete on the most rugged desert terrain imaginable. The most important off-road race is the Mexican 1000—one thousand miles of flat-out racing across the Baja Peninsula in Mexico. In 1971, Parnelli set a record driving-time for the treacherous desert run. Driving a Ford Bronco jeep, he made the run from Tijuana to La Paz, Mexico, in 14 hours and 59 minutes.

This was a far cry from the 34 hours and 45 minutes clocked at the very first Mexican 1000 held in 1967. Parnelli competed again in 1972 and won the race for the second consecutive year, although he did not beat his record of a year before. (The 1972 win was made in 16 hours, 47 minutes, and 35 seconds). Early in 1973, Parnelli won the Baja 500, which is much like the Mexican 1000, except on a smaller scale.

Parnelli Jones fought his way to the top in racing, driving everything from jalopies to Indy cars. Throughout his career he has been talented, daring, and extremely aggressive as a driver. He still is. Apart from managing his Firestone stores and his Ford dealership, Parnelli can be seen in an occasional race, usually an off-road race. If Parnelli Jones is in it, it is bound to be a wild event.

In his Bronco jeep, Parnelli jolts over rugged desert terrain during an off-road race.

RICHARD PETTY

Richard Petty has won more stock-car races than any other driver in the history of stock-car racing. Since he first started racing in 1958, Petty has won more than 150 races and has earned well over one million dollars in prize money. These are record winnings that will surely stand unbeaten for a long time. Beyond a doubt, Richard Petty is stock-car king. The story behind Richard Petty's success actually begins with his father, Lee, and includes his brother, Maurice, and his cousin, Dale Inman.

Richard Petty was born in Level Cross, North Carolina, in 1937. He and Maurice were still young boys when they first started racing. Together they would organize neighborhood bicycle races and then challenge the other kids to beat them. More often than not, one of the Pettys would win. But if not, the winner would usually be their cousin and close friend, Dale Inman.

Richard Petty

The person who really brought racing to the Petty household was the boys' father, Lee. Lee Petty knew a lot about cars, and he shared his knowledge with his sons. He was

Lee Petty

home, Lee Petty thought it would be fun to try. So with Richard, Maurice, and Dale eager to work as his junior pit crew, he entered some stock-car races. He won many of them, too.

During Lee's early racing days, the mid-1940s, stock-car racing was completely disorganized. There was no formal sponsoring organization and no code of rules for stock-car racing. The prize money never amounted to much, either. But worse than that, drivers could never be sure whether the race promoter would pay them after a race or run off with the money himself! Quite naturally, many drivers were unhappy about the way the races were handled. So they decided to do something about it. In 1949, a group of drivers formed the National Association for Stock Car Automobile Racing. The purposes of NASCAR were to organize stock-car races, create a national stock-car championship

always building and modifying cars in the front yard of his home, trying to make them go faster. He didn't race cars himself, but when he saw some stock-car races near his title, and secure more prize money for the drivers. NASCAR races would be open to all American stock cars, and they would be known as Grand National races.

As one of the early members of NASCAR, Lee Petty won his share of races and made the Petty name known. During the early 1950s, Lee became so involved with racing stock cars that he made it his full-time profession. Although Richard and Maurice were still in school, they were always on hand to help their father prepare his car for the races. Weeks ahead of time, the three Pettys would spend the evenings completely rebuilding Lee's car. In the process, every possible modification was made to create more speed in the car and to generally improve its performance. Even at the race track, Richard, Maurice, and Dale would be busy in the pits, working on the car right up until race time. Actually, the boys were too young to be allowed in the pits. So once they got past the guards, they constantly had to hide from speedway officials. In time, the officials granted the boys special passes to the pit area.

After Richard and Maurice graduated from high school, they began to build their father's cars and pit for him on a full-time basis. The boys also helped their father tow his cars to various tracks all over the South, where stock-car racing was especially popular. With the help of his sons, Lee Petty became a very successful driver during those early days of NASCAR. In 1954, he won enough races to capture the Grand National title. Before he retired as a driver in 1962, Lee Petty won the Grand National title again in 1958 and 1959.

It was in 1958 that 21-year-old Richard

Petty decided he wanted to race, too. He entered his first race with NASCAR that year and finished sixth. Though he was eager to prove himself in competition, Richard didn't race very often that first year because he was still helping Maurice and Dale build Lee's cars. But in 1959, Richard traveled the stock-car circuit with his father, frequently competing against him on the tracks. As father and son moved from race to race through the South, they attracted many fans who enjoyed watching the two compete. It was easy to recognize the Pettys on the track. Both drove Plymouths—Lee's was number 42 and Richard's was number 43. And both cars were painted a light blue color that eventually came to be called "Petty Blue."

The 1959 racing season held special significance for Richard, because that was the year

In the early 1960s, Richard Petty was just starting to establish his reputation on the Grand National circuit.

NASCAR named him Rookie of the Year. After being awarded this distinction, Richard decided to leave the car-building to Maurice and Dale so that he could devote all of his time to racing. During the next few years Richard worked hard to improve his driving. His efforts were rewarded on the track when he started finishing ahead of his father in the races. Lee Petty was still the better driver of the two, but everyone realized that Richard was going to be a future champion.

When Lee retired in 1962, he had become something of a legend in stock-car racing. So his son Richard had a real goal to aim for. It wasn't long, however, before Richard proved himself every bit the champion that his father had been. By 1963, Richard Petty had won more than 24 races and had been voted NASCAR's most popular driver by the race fans. A year later, in 1964, he was well on his way to the top. He started the year by winning the most important stock-car race in the world, the Daytona 500. And by the end of the 1964 season, he had won enough races to claim his first Grand National title. Besides receiving these honors, Richard was again voted NASCAR's most popular driver, and Maurice was voted the best mechanic in stock-car racing by NASCAR officials. It was some year for the Petty family! The hard work of past years was starting to pay off.

Richard was the only one in the family who raced after Lee's retirement, but racing continued to be a family affair. Lee managed the business end of the team, while Maurice and Dale built and maintained the cars. And when Richard wasn't racing, he would pitch in and help with the preparation of the cars, too. The situation changed, however, following the 1964 racing season. At that time, an interest in golf began to occupy Lee's time. He finally quit the racing business altogether, leaving Richard, Maurice, and Dale to run the Petty team themselves.

A. J. Foyt—one of racing's
strongest personalities

Richard Petty during a pit stop. In 1973, the sides of his "Petty Blue" Dodge were painted red as part of an advertising agreement with the STP Corporation.

Parnelli Jones in the famed Turbocar. Indianapolis, 1967.

Mark Donohue relaxes in his car
before being wheeled onto the track
for the start of the 1972 Indy 500.

Despite Lee's absence, the years 1965 and 1966 were good ones for the Petty team. Over those two years, Richard won 12 major races (including his second Daytona 500) and earned almost $100,000 in prize money. It was the following year, however, that was to be Richard's greatest in stock-car racing.

Richard Petty was almost unbeatable in 1967, winning 27 out of the 48 races that he entered. During that season, he won 10 consecutive races and earned over $130,000 in prize money. It was the best year that a driver had ever had in the history of Grand National racing.

The "Petty Blue" Plymouth went on to win 16 races in 1968, raking in $90,000 in prize money. But 1968 was also the year that Plymouth decided not to sponsor Richard's stock car again due to financial squabbles. So he had to look for another make of car to drive for the 1969 season. Because of his great reputation, Richard didn't have to look far. Ford had long been trying to persuade him to drive one of their cars, so Richard signed the Petty team with Ford. Number 43 was now, for the first time, a "Petty Blue" *Ford*.

Although 1969 was a successful year for the Petty team, their luck with Fords wasn't as good as it had been with Plymouths. Richard won only 10 races that year for his new sponsor, but he managed to earn over $100,000 in prize money. At the end of the 1969 season, the Plymouth people decided that they wanted the Pettys back under their

Richard Petty lies pinned beneath his car after crashing at the Darlington speedway in 1970. He escaped with only minor injuries.

sponsorship, so Richard returned to driving Plymouths.

In 1970, Richard drove his Plymouth to 18 victories, despite the fact that at the start of the season he had survived the worst accident of his life. It had happened at Darlington, South Carolina, during the Rebel 400 race. As Richard's car came out of a corner, it hit the outside wall and flipped over. The car rolled more than five times, rammed against a concrete wall, and finally came to rest upside down. The car was completely destroyed, but Richard wasn't seriously hurt. His miraculous escape had proved the worth of safety equipment in stock cars.

The accident did not affect Richard's driving ability at all. In fact, Richard Petty went on to establish a new racing record by becoming the first three-time winner of the Daytona 500. His third Daytona victory came at the beginning of the 1971 season. It was really a great way to start the year. And he finished it by winning his third Grand National title.

All through 1972, Richard Petty continued his winning pace. As always, he was assisted in his efforts by Maurice and Dale, the master-builders of the Petty team. By the end of the season, Petty had captured his *fourth* Grand National championship.

The following year, 1973, marked Richard Petty's 15th year in stock-car racing. That spring, after winning at Daytona for the fourth time, Petty's career record stood at over 150 Grand National wins and well over 1 million dollars in prize money. To no one's surprise, Petty returned to Daytona in 1974 for his *fifth* win.

In 16 years, Richard Petty has broken stock-car records for most number of wins in a career, most wins in one season, most money earned in a career, and most money earned in one season. With even *more* wins ahead of him, Richard Petty will remain stock-car king for a long time.

A tired but happy Richard Petty faces his cheering fans after winning the 1973 Daytona 500. Andy Granatelli, then STP president, flashes a victory sign.

A. J. FOYT

Even people who are unfamiliar with auto racing can easily recognize the name A.J. Foyt. A driver and builder of race cars, Foyt is one of the best known men in professional auto racing. It is probably his fierce competitive spirit that has made Foyt such a colorful character in racing. To A.J., winning is everything and second place is nothing. He will race just as hard to win $50 in a midget-car race at some little-known track as he will to win $200,000 at the Indy 500. A.J. Foyt is a "hard-charging" driver and a real winner.

It's easy to see how A.J. Foyt became interested in racing cars. Born in 1935, in Houston, Texas, Anthony Joseph Foyt, Jr., was actually driving a miniature race car around his parents' yard by the time he was three years old. A.J.'s father, Anthony Joseph

A. J. Foyt

Foyt, Sr., was a mechanic and former race-car driver, so there were always plenty of race cars around the Foyt home. When A.J. was five, his father built him a larger car, a midget racer. Young A.J. would race his midget car in exhibition runs that were held between featured races at the local tracks. There, the fearless five-year-old would often reach speeds as high as 50 mph in his racer. All through his school years, A.J. raced any kind of car he could find—midgets, sprints, and stock cars. He wasn't a big winner in competitions, but he did win enough races to make a reputation for himself. A.J. Foyt just seemed to be a natural-born race driver. By the time he left high school, A.J. had made up his mind to become a professional race-car driver.

A.J.'s first full year of big-league racing was 1957, when he was 22 years old. At that time, he was being sponsored by the United States Auto Club and was racing mostly midget cars. Though he didn't finish very high in the championship standings that year, he did manage to win a few races. But, more important, people were beginning to notice Foyt's ability. His "hard-charging" style of driving eventually brought him to the attention of Indy-car owner Al Dean. Dean saw in A.J. a potential champion, so he offered A.J. the wheel of his Indy car, the Dean Van Lines Special, for the 1958 Indy 500.

At Indy, A.J. qualified the car 12th in the starting line-up, and then finished 16th after driving a steady race. It was a disappointing finish for A.J. Although he had hardly expected to win the world's biggest track race

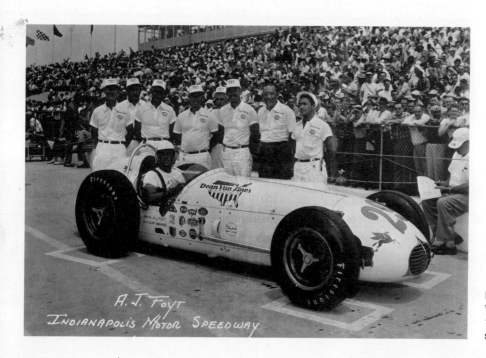

A. J. Foyt
Indianapolis Motor Speedway

Foyt at the wheel of the Dean Van Lines Special, Indianapolis, 1958. Car owner Al Dean stands second from the right.

on his first try, he had expected to do better than *16th*.

By 1959, A.J. was back at Indy and determined to win this time. Starting 17th, he worked his way up to 5th place at one point, but fell back toward the end of the race to finish 10th. It was a better finish than the year before, A.J. knew, but it still wasn't winning. For the remainder of the year, he won a few midget- and sprint-car races, finishing 10th overall in USAC's national championship standings.

In 1960, A.J. was determined to win the national championship title. Winning it would mean that he could have that much-honored number—"1"—painted on his car for the 1961 season. However, the year started badly when A.J. managed to place only 15th at Indy due to mechanical problems in his car. By the end of the year, he had won several races and had placed high enough in the point standings to be one of two major contenders for the title. Besides A.J., the other major contender was two-time Indy winner Roger Ward. Whichever of the two won the last race of the season at Phoenix would win the title.

Early in the Phoenix race, Ward blew the engine in his racer and left the track, no longer in competition for the title. A.J. could afford to slow down at this point and take it easy. But that wasn't A.J.'s style. He kept driving hard anyway, and eventually won the race by more than two laps. A.J. had won his first USAC national driving championship.

A.J. Foyt in the Winner's Circle following his first Indy 500 victory in 1961

In the 1961 season his car would carry the coveted number 1.

If 1960 had been a good year for A.J., 1961 was even better. He started the year by winning his first Indy 500 race. And for the second year in a row, he won the national championship title. A.J. Foyt was now considered a threat in every race he entered, for it was obvious that he was a driver to be reckoned with. It was also obvious that he was a very sore loser. A.J. had a very hot temper, and when he lost a race, he was not at all pleased. Standing five feet eleven and weighing almost 200 pounds, A.J. Foyt looks more like a professional boxer than a race car driver. So when A.J. gets mad, people just stay out of his way.

People were staying out of A.J.'s way in 1962, when he lost the national championship title to his former rival Roger Ward. Just like the year before, winning the championship depended on winning the last race of the season. But in 1962, the last-race victory went to Roger Ward. There was more bad luck for A.J. that year. At Indy, a broken wheel put him out of the race early, and he finished only 23rd. He did win nine other races that season, though. Two of those wins were in stock cars, which A.J. had just started driving again. Winning races in stock cars proved to be just as easy for A.J. as winning races in Indy cars.

In 1963, the Europeans came to Indianapolis with their rear-engined, lightweight cars to challenge the Americans and their heavy, front-engined roadsters. A.J. decided that the European cars were too flimsy and that he would be better off in one of the familiar roadsters. The new rear-engined cars didn't win that year, but neither did A.J. It was Parnelli Jones, driving a roadster, who finished in first place, followed by Jim Clark in one of the European cars. A.J. finished third. Though the new rear-engined lightweights had proved themselves, the American drivers still didn't care for them.

Following Indy that year, A.J. raced sports cars for the first time in his career. At a sports-car race in Nassau, the Bahamas, A.J. won the Governor's Cup over many world-famous road-racing stars. By the end of the season, A.J. had won his third national championship title.

For the 1964 Indy 500, A.J. had a new rear-engined car built for him. But as race time approached, he decided to drive his roadster instead. He had changed his mind because he still believed that the new cars were unsafe. His decision proved to be a wise one, for he went on to win his second Indy 500 that year in the roadster. Continuing his record-breaking season, A.J. won the national

Top: Indy racers were once heavy, front-engine roadsters like this one driven by A.J. Foyt in 1961. *Bottom:* The lightweight, rear-engine racers from Europe became popular at Indianapolis in 1965.

championship for the fourth time. In the few short years that he had been racing, A.J. had set many new racing records.

At the beginning of the 1965 season, A.J. suffered one of the worst accidents of his career. In a stock-car race at the Riverside, California, road course, his car flipped over an embankment and was completely destroyed. A.J. wasn't seriously hurt, but the accident kept him out of racing for several weeks. When he recovered, he went to Indianapolis to try out the new rear-engined car that he had bought for that year's Indy 500. He practiced in the new car, but he still didn't like driving it. Despite his dislike for the car, he qualified it for the pole position. During the actual race, however, the car went out with mechanical problems, forcing him to finish 15th overall. The rest of the year was equally disappointing. Even though A.J. had won several races during the year, it was Mario Andretti who won the championship title at the end of the season.

The following year, 1966, was an all-time low period for A.J. Foyt. Mechanical problems kept him out of contention in every race that he ran, including the Indy 500. And he placed a dismal 13th in the final championship standings for that season.

For the 1967 racing season, A.J. and his father had designed and built an Indy car of their own, called the Coyote. Starting the year off in good fashion, A.J. won the Indy 500 with his new racer. He had now won the Indianapolis 500-mile race *three* times and was the only active driver to have ever done

A big winner in Indy-car and sports-car races, A.J. Foyt is also a hard charger in stock-car events.

this. Shortly after his victory at Indy, A.J. teamed with Dan Gurney to win the famous 24-hour endurance race for sports cars at LeMans, France. And for an incredible *fifth* time, Foyt won the USAC national driving championship at year's end. No other driver in the history of Indy-car racing has come close to beating that record yet. A year later, Foyt won the USAC stock-car title.

Since 1967, when he won his third Indy victory, Foyt's goal has been to win that race for a fourth time. But bad luck has kept him out of the Winner's Circle at Indianapolis. In 1969 his chances looked good because he qualified for the pole position at Indy. Unfortunately, he was forced out of the race due to loss of oil from his car. Foyt's bad luck continued in 1970. That year he finished 10th at Indy after having mechanical problems with his car. A year later, however, things went better, for A.J. finished the 1971 Indy 500 in 3rd place.

During 1971 and 1972, A.J. Foyt was quite busy in stock-car racing. He won NASCAR 500-mile races both at Atlanta, Georgia, and at Ontario, California in 1971. In 1972, he won the Daytona 500 and, for the second consecutive year, the Ontario Miller High Life 500. He finished second in the Texas 500 that year.

At Indianapolis in 1972, Foyt was not successful in his continuing bid for a fourth Indy victory. Mechanical problems once again kept him from it. Later that season, A.J. was involved in a racing accident that kept him out of racing for several weeks. But early in 1973, Foyt was back on the racing scene. In May he won one of the two races in the Trenton 200 series for Indy cars. Foyt's longtime rival Mario Andretti won the other race.

Like other really successful race-car drivers, A.J. Foyt possesses a special attitude toward racing. He is courageous, devoted, and determined to win. In addition, A.J. has a special aggressive quality that is all his own. Foyt also has an inborn skill for race-car driving that has made him one of the truly greats in auto racing. As long as he continues to race, A.J. Foyt will be a ranking contender for every win.

A. J. Foyt drove his "Coyote" in an unsuccessful try at the 1973 Indy 500. In 1974, the car started in the pole position but failed to finish due to engine trouble.

MARK DONOHUE

Mark Donohue has been another highly successful American race car driver. Most of his successes have been in road racing, but he has also done well in track racing. In addition to his driving skill, Mark's college training in engineering has also been a great help to his career. He really understands what makes racing cars go, and he is able to take part in their design and development. Because of his abilities as both a driver and an engineer, Mark Donohue has become one of the most respected figures in the world of auto racing.

Mark Donohue was born in Summit, New Jersey, in 1937. Even as a boy, he was interested in cars. But it wasn't until 1959, when he graduated from Brown University with a degree in mechanical engineering, that he really became involved with cars. After his graduation, Mark joined the Sports Car Club of America and decided to enter one of its

Mark Donohue

hillclimbing competitions. The hill-climb was the first automobile competition that he had ever entered, and he won it in his Corvette. The event hooked him on racing for good.

With a racing career in mind, Mark Donohue scraped together enough money to buy an Elva sports car. He then entered a driving school for beginning race-car drivers at the Marlboro Raceway in Maryland. After completing the course, Mark was given a SCCA competition license, which allowed him to race in SCCA-sponsored races. In his first race, Mark managed to finish fourth. But he went on from there to win 15 races in a row. These events were all regional races, and they served to prepare Mark for the SCCA national events. In the national races, drivers earn points toward the national championship competition, depending on how well they finish in each event. If they gain enough points to qualify for the national championship competition, they race other cars in their class in a series of races that leads to the national championship title.

Mark entered his first national race in 1961, winning it over the favored driver. After that win, Mark spent the summer towing his Elva around the country to other national races. He drove hard during those months to earn points toward the championship title. By the end of the 1961 season, Mark had won the national championship in the E Production class.

In the same year, Donohue sold his Elva and bought a Formula C car. He did well with the car, until early in the 1962 season, when he broke the car's chassis at a race in Sebring, Florida. At this point, Mark almost quit racing. His car was unusable, and he

Mark Donohue in sports-racing
competition at Sebring, Florida

just didn't have the money to repair it. So, for most of the summer of 1962, Mark gave up racing. A few months later, however, the company that had built his car heard of his problem and sent Mark new automobile parts. Getting these parts was the best possible thing that could have happened to Mark, for it enabled him to get back into racing. During the following two years, he raced a Daimler sports car—without too much success—in addition to other makes of sports cars. He did manage to win a few races in a friend's Cobra, though.

The year 1965 turned out to be the best year of Mark Donohue's career so far. Mark successfully raced a Lotus Formula C car and also a Mustang B Production model. By the end of the season, he had driven *both* of the cars to national championships. These victories started Mark Donohue on the road to professional race-car driving.

Following Mark's spectacular 1965 showing, driver Walt Hangsen invited him to join the Road Racing Driver's Club, a social group for race drivers. This invitation was quite an honor for Mark, because Walt was a very famous driver at the time. The two men soon became great friends. In fact, it was Walt Hangsen who gave Mark his first chance at big-time professional racing. Walt did this by persuading the Ford Motor Company to let Mark and him co-drive one of the big Ford GTs at the 12-hour endurance race at Sebring, Florida. The two drivers did well together at Sebring, and Mark learned a lot about driving from Walt in the process. Tragically, Walt Hangsen was killed later that year, while testing a race car in France. After Walt's death, Mark once again thought of quitting. Late in 1966, however, car-builder

Mark Donohue and Roger Penske

Roger Penske approached Donohue and asked him to drive his cars. After some thought, Mark accepted Penske's offer. That was the beginning of one of the greatest partnerships in the history of racing.

Donohue drove this Chevrolet-powered McLaren car in both the 1966-67
United States Road Racing Championship series and the Can-Am series.

During his first year of driving the Penske cars, Mark won one of the races in the famed Canadian-American Challenge Cup series, beating some of the best drivers in the world.

And he finished second overall in the final standings. Roger Penske knew he had made an excellent choice in partners.

In 1967, Roger entered his cars in the

Can-Am and the United States Road Racing Championship (USRRC) series. The USRRC was open to the same powerful sports cars that competed in the Can-Am, but only American drivers were eligible to race. Mark drove a Lola sports car and completely dominated the USRRC in 1967, winning it easily. The same year, the Penske-Donohue team finished fourth overall in the Can-Am series.

In 1968, Mark and Roger really had their hands full. That year, they decided to go after the championships in three series—the Can-Am and USRRC, and a new series for small American sedans, the Trans-American Sedan Championship. In the USRRC series, Mark repeated his performance of the previous year and won the title for the second time. In the Can-Am, he brought his Lola into third place overall—a slight improvement from the year before. But the really amazing achievement was his success in the new Trans-Am series. Mark won the Trans-Am title that year by driving the Penske Camaro to victory in 12 out of 13 races!

In 1969, Penske and Donohue decided that the past season had been too busy; too much time and money had been spent maintaining several cars and transporting them across the country for three series. So in 1969 the team decided to race in only the Trans-Am and, for the first time, the Indianapolis 500. The team also planned to enter a Lola sports car in some long-distance races. Their plans worked out well. Driving the Penske Camaro, Mark again won the Trans-Am Championship. He also won the 24-hour endurance race for sports cars at Daytona, Florida. As for the Indy 500, neither Mark nor Roger had ever been involved in any kind of oval-track racing before. But, as usual, the team did great.

A thoughtful Mark Donohue waits while his crew tries to locate a mechanical problem during his 1969 Indy 500 run.

Mark qualified the Penske Indy car in the fourth starting position and finished seventh in the race. For this amazing first-time performance, Mark was voted Rookie of the Year by the Indy officials.

By 1970, Mark and Roger had switched to Javelins for the Trans-Am series. The Javelins couldn't touch the performance of the Camaros and Fords that year, but Mark managed to finish second in the Trans-Am, behind the Mustangs. The team did much better at the 1970 Indy 500, however. Mark drove a fine race and finished in second place. Near the end of the summer, he and Roger decided to enter three of SCCA's L&M Continental 5000 races for Formula A cars. Mark won two of them and finished third in the other one.

In 1971, Roger Penske decided to run the Javelins again, even though the team hadn't had much success with them the year before. It turned out to be a good decision, for the

Mark Donohue races his Javelin to victory in the first race of the 1971
Trans-Am series. He finished the entire series in first place that year.

team won the 1971 Trans-Am. After that victory, Mark entered more championship-car races, and he did well in them. But victory in the 500 still eluded him.

The year 1972 started out in a big way for Mark Donohue and Roger Penske. After years of trying, Mark finally won the Indy 500, driving Roger's McLaren championship car. The team also returned to the Can-Am series that year with a new and super-fast Porsche sports car. In the first race of the Can-Am series, Mark led all the way, until a minor

Running neck and neck, Donohue (66) and Peter Revson (12) compete for the 1972 Indy 500 win.

part in the car broke. But he managed to fix it and finish second. Then, at Road Atlanta for the second race of the Can-Am series, Mark crashed his Porsche into a dirt embankment during practice. The car was completely destroyed, and Mark suffered a badly broken leg. Because of the injury to his leg, Mark was unable to race for most of the 1972 season.

When he did return to the tracks late in 1972, Mark attempted a different category of racing —stock-car racing. By the end of the season, he was participating in NASCAR's Grand National series and doing well.

Just *how* well was witnessed early in 1973, when Donohue won his first Grand National victory, the Winston Western 500. Held at the Riverside, California, road course, the Winston Western 500 happened to be the only big-league race on NASCAR's 1973 Grand National calendar. By winning this race, Mark Donohue had won the major stock-car race of the year after only one season in stock-car racing. And he had even won it over the stock-car king himself, Richard Petty!

By the fall of 1973, Mark Donohue felt he had achieved everything he had ever wanted to achieve in racing. So in October, following the last race of the 1973 Can-Am series, Donohue announced his retirement. Though he would no longer be driving, Mark planned to remain active in racing through his business partnership with Roger Penske and the Penske racing enterprise. The Donohue-Penske combination has long been one of the most successful, most respected partnerships in racing. And there is every indication that the team's success will continue for a long time to come.

Mark Donohue in Victory Lane at Indianapolis

THE RACING BOOKS

DRAG RACING
ICE RACING
MOTORCYCLE RACING
ROAD RACING
SNOWMOBILE RACING
TRACK RACING
AMERICAN RACE CAR DRIVERS
INTERNATIONAL RACE CAR DRIVERS
THE INDIANAPOLIS 500

*We specialize in publishing quality books for
young people. For a complete list please write:*

 Lerner Publications Company

241 First Avenue North, Minneapolis, Minnesota 55401